General editor: Graham Handley M

Brodie's Notes on Harold Brighouse's
Hobson's Choice

W. S. Bunnell MA FCP
Headmaster, The Queen's School, Bushey

Pan Books London and Sydney

This revised edition published 1988
by Pan Books Ltd
Cavaye Place, London SW10 9PG
9 8 7 6 5 4 3 2 1
© W. S. Bunnell 1988
ISBN 0 330 50264 6

Photoset by Rowland Phototypesetting Ltd
Bury St Edmunds, Suffolk

Printed and bound in Great Britain by Richard Clay Ltd
Bungay, Suffolk

Extracts from *Hobson's Choice*
are reproduced by kind permission
of Samuel French Ltd.
All rights whatsoever in the play are
fully protected and applications for
performances etc. must be
made in advance to:
Samuel French Ltd.,
52, Fitzroy Street,
London W1P 6JR

Contents

Page references in these Notes are to the edition of the play published by Heinemann Educational Books, but as references are also given to particular Acts, the Notes may be used with any edition of the play.

Preface

The intention throughout this study aid is to stimulate and guide, to encourage the reader's *involvement* in the text, to develop disciplined critical responses and a sure understanding of the main details.

Brodie's Notes provide a summary of the plot of the play or novel followed by act, scene or chapter summaries, each of which will have an accompanying critical commentary designed to emphasize the most important literary and factual details. Poems, stories or non-fiction texts will combine brief summary with critical commentary on either individual aspects or sequences of the genre being considered. Textual notes will be explanatory or critical (sometimes both), defining what is difficult or obscure on the one hand, or stressing points of character, style, plot or the technical aspects of poetry on the other. Revision questions will be set at appropriate points to test the student's careful application to the text of the prescribed book.

The second section of each of these study aids will consist of a critical examination of the author's art. This will cover such major elements as characterization, style, structure, setting, theme(s) for example in novels, plays or stories; in poetry it will deal with the types of poem, rhyme, rhythm, free verse for example, or in non-fiction with the main literary concerns of the work. The editor may choose to examine any aspect of the book being studied which he or she considers to be important. The paramount aim is to send the student back to the text. Each study aid will include a series of general questions which require detailed knowledge of the set book: the first of these questions will have notes by the editor of what *might* be included in a written answer. A short list of books considered useful as background reading for the student will be provided at the end.

The General Certificate of Secondary Education in Literature

These study aids are suitable for candidates taking the new GCSE examinations in English Literature since they provide detailed preparation for examinations in that subject as well as presenting critical ideas and commentary of major use to candidates preparing their coursework files. These aids provide a basic, individual and imaginative response to the appreciation of literature. They stimulate disciplined habits of reading, and they will assist the responsive student to analyse and to write about the texts with discrimination and insight.

Graham Handley

The author and his work

Harold Brighouse was born on 26 July 1882 at Eccles, near Manchester. His mother, before her marriage, had been a headmistress, and his father was in the cotton business. He won a scholarship to Manchester Grammar School, partly as a result of his mother's coaching. At school, he was lazy: he tolerated Latin, disliked Greek and it soon became obvious that he was not going to gain academic distinction. He left school in 1899 to become a learner at a textiles export merchant's in Whitworth Street, Manchester. During this time he became an enthusiastic attender at the Royal Theatre. He was sent to his firm's London Office in 1902 and moved into Mecklenburgh Square. Again he spent much of his time at the theatre as a 'first-nighter' in the gallery. His salary at the age of twenty was £150 a year: the cost of a seat in the gallery was one shilling.

Brighouse wrote a play in five acts which he sent to one of the great actors of the day, Sir Johnston Forbes-Robertson (1853–1937) who, however, returned it, pointing out that its acting time was less than an hour. Brighouse rewrote it as a one-act play, *Lonesome-like*, which he regarded as his best play of this type. He sold it for five pounds in 1911, an unhappy step since it ran to over three thousand performances. At this time he was still working. All his writing was done in the evenings and on Saturdays and Sundays; and, though he possibly did not realize it at the time, he was later to admit that it was through this early constant play-going that he learned the elements of his 'trade'.

Though he continued to live in London, Brighouse remained all his life closely connected with his native Lancashire: from 1913 to 1945 he was a regular contributor to *The Manchester Guardian*. Another great influence was Miss Annie Horniman, who had been connected with the Abbey Theatre in Dublin. In 1908 she bought the Comedy Theatre in Manchester, renamed it the Gaiety, and opened it as a repertory theatre. Miss Horniman was an eccentric spinster whose richly embroidered evening clothes attracted much attention. She considered that a city that could support a weekly concert by the Hallé Orchestra could also support a theatre given over to serious plays. There she established what became known as the 'Manchester School' of playwrights; of these Brighouse and Stanley Houghton (author of *Hindle Wakes*) were the most famous. Allan Monkhouse was another. Under Annie Horniman's rule the theatre in Manchester became a significant influence on English drama. Some, although by no means all, of the plays were based on Lancashire life and habits. The Gaiety survived as a theatre until 1921.

Even when an old man, Brighouse still paid tribute to Miss Horniman and the Manchester School, who inspired him to write *Hobson's Choice*. However, the play opened not in Manchester but in New York, in 1915, after a tour of American towns. It was an immediate success. Whitford Kane who played the part of Willie Mossop said that 'the criticisms read like an actor's dream'. In London it was performed under wartime conditions when people looked to the theatre for light amusement rather than drama. With daily matinees and only two evening performances a week, the play reached 240 performances at the Apollo and Prince of Wales Theatres.

The play was Brighouse's greatest success. He later wrote: 'Only by exceptional merit, almost only once-in-a-lifetime merit, can a regional play overcome London's Mayfair prejudices.' When Brighouse died, *The Times* headed its obituary notice: 'Author of *Hobson's Choice*'.

The play has remained a constant favourite, especially with repertory and amateur companies, and it came to the rescue of the Liverpool Repertory Theatre in 1922. It was at the Liverpool Playhouse that Brighouse thought it had seen its final production, but the play was revived in London in 1952 at the Arts Theatre. Harold Brighouse considered that *Hobson's Choice* was a refutation of the idea that the Manchester school produced 'drab-minded practitioners of excessive naturalism'. He was particularly delighted when it was produced in 1951 at the Grand Theatre in Blackpool (the Lancashire seaside holiday resort), with Wilfred Pickles as Willie Mossop. The production of the play there was an answer to those who equated the Manchester school with serious and miserable social plays.

Naturalism was not peculiar to the Manchester school. Brighouse pointed out that Tennessee Williams wrote at a much later date 'Manchester school' plays in naturalistic style, which would have horrified a Manchester audience of forty years ago.

In 1917 when his father died, Brighouse settled in Hampstead. 'The Heath,' he wrote, 'with its ponds, is my residential Lake District.'

He continued to write. Yet never again was he to repeat anything like the success of *Hobson's Choice*. 'I was formed,' he wrote, 'before the 1914 War, I survived creatively the nineteen-twenties, I wilted in the nineteen-thirties.' He tried his hand at everything – fantasies, farce, comedies, melodrama, grotesque. Many of them were one-act plays, and generally these are the most successful. 'Houghton and I,' he asserted, 'are one-act play men.'

But Brighouse also wrote several full-length plays: among these were: *Garside's Career* (1914); *The Clock Goes Round* (1916); *The Northerners* and *Other Times* (both 1920); *Mary's John* (1920); *What's Bred in the Bone* (1927); *It's a Gamble* (1928) – a comparative failure in the theatre; and *The Sort-of-Prince* (1929). Nearly all of these were Northern comedies.

Then there was the one-act comedy, *Fossie for Short* (1927), adapted from his novel of the same name. *Dealing in Futures* was first produced in Glasgow in 1909, then shown on television in 1960. Some of Brighouse's plays were topical, as their titles suggest: for example, *Air-Raid Refugees* (1939) was based on the Munich crisis.

Brighouse also wrote a number of novels, one in collaboration with Charles Forrest, based on *Hobson's Choice*. He also turned Stanley Houghton's *Hindle Wakes* into a novel.

He did not revolutionize the drama of his day: he was a workmanlike rather than an inspired writer. He confessed that he had no 'lust for self-expression', and that if that was what art was about he was no artist. 'We were of our time,' he wrote, 'influenced by Shaw and by Ibsen's social plays.' His important contribution to the theatre is *Hobson's Choice*, with its Lancashire background, its rich characterization and its humour.

Brighouse considered that, in the words of the Lancashire song, he had reason to be thankful 'for what A've 'ad'. He died in London on 25 July 1958, on the day before his seventy-sixth birthday.

The contemporary theatre

The nineteenth century was a time of greatness in the novel and in poetry. Its drama was abysmal. The early twentieth century represented a new beginning in drama, not the development of an established tradition.

The Norwegian dramatist Henrik Ibsen had shown that plays could be used as a vehicle for serious social purpose. Ibsen's plays are set in the grim reality of Norwegian life as he saw it. In his plays the human spirit is imprisoned within the narrow social morality of bourgeois standards which destroy his heroes and heroines. His main, and perhaps only clear, influence was upon Bernard Shaw. Yet Shaw brought to the grimness of Ibsen a sense of fun and an irrepressible wit. In this he was close to Oscar Wilde who had shown in a series of brilliant comedies that plays could be witty, entertaining and touch lightly on social problems. This is one thread of a tradition that is clearly seen in *Hobson's Choice*: the emphasis on amusing and occasionally extravagant dialogue almost for its own sake.

Shaw had taken as his theme serious social problems: prostitution in *Mrs Warren's Profession* or slum landlords in *Widowers' Houses*. Dramatists such as Harley Granville-Barker and John Galsworthy wrote plays, whose main emphasis is on social problems. *Strife* (1909) is an attempt to explore the harshness of the industrial revolution and *Justice* (1910) of the contemporary legal scene. Unlike Wilde, Shaw and Brighouse, Galsworthy was utterly serious in his social purpose. He established realism of setting as a part of the tradition of the contemporary theatre. Although the treatment of the setting of *Hobson's Choice* is very different from that of Galsworthy, the Salford background is realistic enough.

A central influence on Brighouse is the development of the provincial theatre and settings. This was to reach its full glory in the Irish theatrical movement in which W. B. Yeats and J. M. Synge were to play a leading part as dramatists. This movement was to have as its home the Abbey Theatre in Dublin, funded by Miss Annie Horniman who was heiress to the Horniman tea fortune.

Before establishing the Dublin theatre, she had begun the repertory theatre in Manchester at the Gaiety Theatre and the seasons of plays produced here ran from 1908 to 1921. Playwrights associated with

Miss Horniman's theatre came to be referred to as belonging to the 'Manchester School' of drama. One of the dramatists who contributed to these seasons was William Stanley Houghton who became famous through his play *Hindle Wakes* (1912). The story is about a young man's advances to a girl employed by his father. Marriage is the only possible solution. The play is unusual because it is the girl who refuses to marry a lover that she would despise as a husband. The girl Fanny Hawthorn's defiant rejection of social convention is akin to Maggie Hobson's independence in her selection of Willie Mossop in *Hobson's Choice*.

In his autobiography Brighouse mentions his frequent theatre visits in Manchester and later in London where at the Court Theatre in Sloane Square he saw the plays of Granville-Barker. Although Brighouse cannot be specifically categorized as belonging to the Manchester movement, he, like Houghton, is now chiefly known for his contribution to drama in a local Lancashire setting. *Hobson's Choice* is an outstanding example. The Manchester movement was limited in time and achievement; it produced neither the dramatists nor the quality of plays that mark the Irish theatre.

Plot

The plot of *Hobson's Choice* is basically an account of the rise of William Mossop and the downfall of Henry Horatio Hobson, whose eldest daughter Maggie is the key to the movement of the plot.

There is, of course, nothing revolutionary here. Rags to riches was not only a Victorian myth; it was frequently an actuality: marrying the master's daughter was one way of achieving it. The only unusual aspect is Maggie's early part in the scheme. Shaw, however, in his play *Man and Superman* in 1903, published thirteen years before the production of *Hobson's Choice*, had explored the theme that it is woman who pursues man. There was doubtless, in Victorian times as in all other times, a breed of dominating women who ruled those around them. Lady Bracknell in Oscar Wilde's *The Important of Being Earnest*, produced in 1895, would have proved an interesting adversary for Maggie in the art of domination. And the eventual reversal of roles between Maggie and Willie is not new: Shakespeare's *Taming of the Shrew* is a famous example on that theme.

Indeed, the plot in *Hobson's Choice* is neither shot through with original ideas and incidents nor is it particularly exciting in itself. Brighouse excels not so much in the development of a continuous story as in the creation of a series of incidents that illustrate the richness and humour of character. 'Character must have something to be characteristic about – in one word, plot,' Brighouse stated. Indeed one critic of the film of *Hobson's Choice*, made in 1953, complained that it too obviously exploited certain set pieces in the play. It is incident, people, background and humour that the audience will remember: the plot is a vehicle for these.

The plot contains elements of both comedy and farce. The word farce is used to classify a play whose total purpose is to move the audience to laughter. This is often achieved through the creation of absurd situations at the expense of any convincing characterization. There is usually an abundance of physical action, such as falling over, exchanging blows, tearing clothes.

There is clearly little of this in *Hobson's Choice*. Situations are commonly amusing because of the characters who participate in them. The audience does not see Hobson falling into the cellar as they would in farce, and the humour of the situation lies in the contrast between Hobson's self-importance and his lying there sleeping off the effects of drink. The more outrageous situations between Willie and Maggie still spring convincingly out of their respective characters and their relationship.

Comedy is a more delicate and sophisticated affair than farce. Although the principal aim of both is to amuse, comedy does this in a more intellectual way. Molière, the great French writer of comedies, defined the purpose of comedy as depicting the ridiculous aspects of men and women, and this is a principal aim of *Hobson's Choice*. Comedy must never sacrifice character to a situation that arouses laughter. This is a boundary that Brighouse is careful to observe. The humour springs from what is said rather than what is done.

The play in the cinema

A film was made of *Hobson's Choice* in 1963 (British Lion). It is a brilliant version of the play directed by David Lean. The leading parts are outstandingly portrayed by Charles Laughton (Hobson), Brenda de Banzie (Maggie) and John Mills (Willie Mossop). A film was also produced in 1931 by Thomas Bentley from a screenplay by Frank Launder with James Harcourt, Viola Lyel and Frank Pettingell in the main roles.

Act summaries, critical comments, textual notes and revision questions

Act 1

The scene is Hobson's Boot Shop in Chapel Street, Salford. The workroom is in a cellar, below the shop, and is reached by a trap door. The year is 1880. The shop is successful, but nothing is elaborate. Behind the counter are Hobson's two younger daughters, Alice and Victoria. Maggie, Hobson's eldest daughter, enters.

The three daughters discuss their father's late rising. It is clear that he is still recovering from his drinking of the previous evening. Alice is anxious to have the place to herself, as she is expecting a visit from Albert Prosser. Albert enters and is intercepted by Maggie who, much against his will, sells him a pair of boots.

Hobson now enters and proceeds to lecture his daughters threatening to marry off the two youngest if they do not mend their ways. As for Maggie, he tells her that she is an old maid with no hopes of marrying.

As Hobson leaves, a valued and wealthy customer arrives to inquire who made a particularly pleasing pair of boots. Hobson grumbles at a workman being praised.

Jim Heeler, Hobson's drinking companion, arrives and Hobson opens his heart to him on a widower's problems in handling three grown-up daughters. Jim advises Hobson to get them married. However, Hobson's enthusiasm for this scheme quickly cools when he hears that he would be expected to provide a marriage settlement for each daughter.

When Hobson has gone out, Maggie summons Willie to come to speak to her. Willie is content with his station in life and with his work at Hobson's. Maggie proposes marriage to Willie, and says what a good working partnership they would make. Maggie would be an excellent seller and Willie a splendid workman. However, he points out that he is not in love with her; he is also engaged to Ada Figgins. Maggie regards the weak helpless Ada as totally unsuitable for Willie.

When Ada, whose appearance reflects her colourless personality, enters with Willie's dinner, Maggie bluntly tells her that she intends to marry Willie. Ada is no match for Maggie, not even with Willie's half-hearted support.

Maggie intends that the marriage shall take place in three weeks. Alice and Vickey are dismayed when they hear of the engagement; so is Hobson when he returns. Hobson threatens to strap Willie but as he swings the strap, Willie shows a new resolution: he kisses Maggie, and pledges his future to her.

Commentary

A dramatist must face up to three problems at the beginning of a play. He must arouse the audience's interest in the story by the rapid introduction of incident; he must introduce the characters, and, in comedy, they should be easily recognizable types; he must sketch vividly and convincingly the setting, period and atmosphere of the play. In this third problem the stage and its set will assist the audience. The shop with its clogs, boots and slippers, its boot boxes, and its counter indicate the setting before a word is spoken.

Maggie is introduced immediately because she, along with Hobson and Mossop, is going to be one of the three leading characters throughout the play. Maggie is the prime mover of the plot. The sequence of events is largely dominated by Maggie's personality and her clear-sighted vision of what she wants to happen. The brief interlude with Albert establishes her personality and her controlling influence not only in the shop but over the lives of the other characters and what will happen to them.

Hobson does not appear immediately and, when he does, there is a heightened expectation and a sharpening of interest in the audience as the struggle for supremacy between him and Maggie begins. Plot and character in this, as in all good plays, are inextricably related. Between such well-defined, vital and wilful characters the battle is going to be titanic. The audience is already engaged.

The atmosphere is solidly Victorian lower middle class. There is no air of aristocratic leisure or luxury here. The family are all workers. Their prosperity is dependent on the success of the shop. Yet they are conscious of their position. Employers and employed belong to different social worlds. Maggie's intention to marry Willie Mossop is a revolutionary and startling affront to a class-conscious society, where parents felt entitled to institute serious and prolonged inquiries into the financial and social background of any prospective partner. Hobson is a representative of the established order of society. He knows that his position in it is conditioned by his financial standing. His way is not to earn more but to spend less. Whilst Maggie is creative, thrusting, ready to exploit assets such as her own sales ability and Willie Mossop's craftsmanship, Hobson wants to conserve what he has; he is mean towards his daughters; he is limited in his ideas about the shop.

The characters are vigorously portrayed in the very beginning. Their traits, however, are strongly and simply drawn. This is the world of comedy, and the audience needs to have a clear idea of the characters and their relationships as a framework for the development of the play's humour. This is not to say that the characters are stereotypes who do not develop: they do. Willie Mossop is manifestly a character who is going to develop abundantly as the play unfolds. This is predictable and not unexpected. It is a transformation that the audience anticipates with lively curiosity before the end of the first act.

The first act in its characterization and its humour exploits contrasts. Maggie is contrasted with Hobson and her two sisters, Willie Mossop with Albert Prosser, Mrs Hepworth's evaluation of Willie with that of Hobson, Maggie's idea of marriage with that of her sisters, Hobson's concept of his own importance with the reality. This is often expressed in small things. The conflict between Hobson and Maggie finds its expression in the time that dinner is to be served, that between Hobson and Alice and Vickey by the argument about the sort of dresses they have been wearing. The conflict is serious but its expression is humorous. This is the source of the play's rich comedy, the close relationship between character and situation. The situations in the first act are amusing in themselves, but an extra dimension is given to the comedy because of the characters who are taking part. The audience enjoys seeing Hobson and Maggie and Willie in these situations; there is a sense of sympathy and identification that causes us to laugh rather with than at the characters. The level of identification differs; the audience will start to side with Maggie and Willie rather than Hobson. But there is no malice towards him. The audience forgives him his meanness because it is a rich source of amusement.

By the end of the first act the characters are well established. The audience, amused, interested and sympathetic, looks forward to the development of the plot in the second act.

Hobson's Choice This means having no choice at all. The saying comes from a Thomas Hobson (c. 1544-1631) who had a stable in Cambridge. His customers were allowed no choice of horse but had to take each animal in turn. The reference is to the end of the play, where the Salford Hobson is given no choice about his future and no say in the arrangements.

Salford An industrial town separated from Manchester only by the River Irwell, formerly a centre of the cotton industry. In the Victorian times in which the play is set, Salford combined, in terms of housing and working conditions, some of the worst conditions inherited from the Industrial Revolution, with a fierce civic pride, expressed in its public buildings. Life there was not easy.

Clogs These were the normal footwear of the Salford working class.

masonic emblems Badges worn by the Freemasons, a society for mutual help and the promotion of brotherly feeling, with exclusive rituals and a system of secret signs. The masons are organized into lodges; in some circles being a mason is regarded as a social cachet.

carriage folk Those who owned carriages were the well-to-do section of society.

leathering Thrashing, originally with a leather thong.

John Bright (1811–89) Liberal politician, famed as an orator. With Cobden, he led the agitation for the repeal of the Corn Laws. He was deeply opposed to warfare, denouncing the Crimean War and Gladstone's Egyptian policy. He was a Rochdale man, and a social reformer.

windbag A man who talks a lot but means, and does, little.

moithered Bothered (Dialect).

temperance The temperance movement was important at the time. Its aim was to remove the social abuses that resulted from excessive drinking, by encouraging the adoption of teetotalism. This is an ironic comment on Hobson's expectations and his own habits.

get my hand down Dip into my pocket, be generous.

warm Well-off (Dialect).

Settlements A sum of money or property given on marriage.

tokened Engaged (Dialect).

hold your hush Be quiet (Dialect).

jaw Talk at (Dialect).

workhouse brat A child born in a workhouse (a place of refuge for the down-and-out) and therefore, to someone like Hobson, the lowest of the low.

brass Money (Dialect).

gradely Fine (Dialect).

Revision questions on Act 1

1 Describe Hobson's relationship to his daughters as revealed in Act 1.

2 What does the opening of the play show of the character of Maggie?

3 Describe and comment on Hobson's view of women and their place in the home.

4 What impression is given of Willie in Act 1?

5 Ada and Mrs Hepworth represent opposite poles of character. Discuss.

Act 2

The setting is the shop at midday. Vickey is, as usual, reading. Alice is struggling with the ledgers. Vickey reveals to Alice that there is someone she too would like to marry.

Maggie enters the shop, followed by Freddy Beenstock (the man of Vickey's choice). Then Willie enters. It is Maggie's wedding day; she tells Freddy to fetch Albert to the shop. Hobson is out of the way because, as they have learned from Freddy, he has fallen down a cellar trap at the Beenstock's corn warehouse. Hobson is unhurt, but snoring soundly.

Maggie insists that her two sisters accept Willie as one of the family and then announces that she is going to do something about getting her sisters married.

Albert produces the paper on which an action is drawn up against Hobson for trespass on the property of Beenstock and Company, damages to certain corn bags and further damages for spying on their business. Maggie instructs Freddy to place this paper on Hobson as he lies snoring in their cellar.

Albert is dragooned into pushing the handcart which Maggie and Willie have brought to collect their furniture; he is appalled at the idea, but does it.

Commentary

This act is a consolidation. It adds little to the knowledge of the characters. The act is the presentation of a moment in time that takes place a month after the opening act. Striking events have taken place before the act begins: the audience is made more aware of this because the changed situation is presented as a fact, a translation into reality of Maggie's vision and determination.

Maggie is even more vital and exhibits perhaps an even greater dominance over situations and people than she showed in the first act. Maggie has exploded into her true self, and she sails through the act with an exuberance that reduces the other characters to pale caricatures. This is a possible weakness. Perhaps Maggie's triumph is just a little too overwhelmingly complete. The first act was based on the comedy springing from the weakness of human beings; the second act lurches towards the situation of farce. The humour springing from the image of Albert's pushing a hand-cart loaded with lumber through the streets of Salford springs from a superficial picture of Albert. Nevertheless it is amusing: that is enough in the world of comedy.

The audience has to draw conclusions. The changed situation presented is not explained. This arouses an active curiosity. There is also an economy of narrative that is impressive and highly effective.

Hobson does not appear in this act, but he is part of the movement towards farce. Hobson's pompous self-importance has taken a fall into Freddy's cellar. Yet the comedy here is two-dimensional. The picture of Hobson lying there asleep in his drunken stupor is not only amusing in itself, it also provides a situation that Maggie can exploit for her own ends. This link between character and plot raises the incident above farce.

The theme of class continues and is sharpened in this act. The pretensions of Alice and Vickey are shown to be shallow: the decline of the business also shows their social aims to be dangerously lacking in substance, something that is underlined by their own lack of competence. They have the occasional flashes of fire, but they are a little too stereotyped and shadowy to be fully amusing.

Although there has been a significant shift in circumstance during this act, the audience must regard it as something of an interlude. It is predictable from what the audience has learned from the first act, and the consequences of it point to the next act.

In the original published edition there were only three acts, though it has always been performed as four. Brighouse noted that he preferred to print the play in three acts as he originally intended. This act was the first scene of the second act.

play old Harry Be angry and shout (Dialect).
nowty Uncertain, irritable (Dialect).
blood Dandy, man about town.
shape Do something about it (Dialect).
lief Willingly (Dialect).
Flat Iron Market A market selling second-hand goods including furniture.
horsehair Hair from the mane and tail of a horse; much used in Victorian times for stuffing mattresses, leather chairs and sofas etc.

Revision questions on Act 2

1 What does this act reveal of the characters of Alice and Vickey?

2 The chief purpose of this act is to further the plot. How far is this true? What developments are made in the plot?

3 What social attitudes are revealed in Act 2?

4 How far does Maggie's attitude to her wedding day reflect her previous views of marriage?

Act 3

The setting is the cellar in Oldfield Road.

Seated on the sofa are Albert, Alice, Vickey and Freddy. They stand to toast 'The Bride and Bridegroom'.

Willie nervously makes a speech and does astonishingly well – Maggie has been educating him.

Hobson knocks, to the consternation of everyone except Maggie. She ushers them all into the bedroom except Willie. Maggie makes it very obvious, even before Hobson enters, that Willie is to act as the master of the house.

Hobson brings out the action for damages for trespass; he sees financial ruin and the destruction of his respectability yawning before him. He lays the blame at Maggie's door. It is her marriage that has driven him to drink and to this lapse. Willie means to offer comfort, but he is very much the voice of doom to Hobson. Maggie advises her father to settle out of court. She calls Albert in – to Hobson's amazement. Vickey, Alice and Freddy then come into the room. Hobson begins by abusing lawyers in general and Albert in particular; Albert suggests settling at one thousand pounds. At this point Maggie intervenes to say that one thousand is too much; she states that five hundred pounds is what her father can afford and that is what he will pay.

Maggie informs a puzzled Hobson that the money will not be going out of the family; the money, she explains, will be used as marriage settlements for Vickey and Alice. Hobson turns on Maggie accusing her of being the cause of all this. He is sorry for Willie in having her for a wife. He warns the two young men of the pains of marriage.

Before retiring to bed, Maggie has to fetch Willie – by his ear.

Commentary

This act represents the climax of the play. The commonest theme of comedy is the problems lovers have in coming together in marriage, and its resolution lies in the removal of the obstacles and the solution of the problems. This is what happens during this act. From one wedding – Maggie and Willie's – flow two more marriages. The problem lies not in the relationships of the two couples, although some of Alice's comments during the speeches reveal that Albert may have his problems once he is married, but in getting Hobson's agreement. This provides the substance of the act in terms of the plot. Maggie continues the exploitation of the situation in which Hobson found himself in Act 2.

The tension arises not from whether Hobson will agree but from the interplay of characters in the struggle. There is a revival of the glorious interplay of situation and character that was a mark of the first act. The situation brings out all Hobson's characteristics: his fear of the loss of his reputation, the reporting of his misdemeanours not only in the local Salford press but in *The Manchester Guardian* where the whole of Lancashire can read and enjoy his downfall, is the ultimate dilemma for Hobson, enshrined firmly in his middle-class values. He is a man tortured and stretched on the rack. Yet it is squarely set within the bounds of comedy. There is a solution. His reputation can be saved but at the cost of his pocket. Hobson has to weigh against each other his two cardinal values – reputation and money. The conflict provides excellent humour.

There is no viciousness in this comedy. Even Hobson is not to be punished too harshly. Maggie is there to ensure that excessive demands are not made on him. Comic suffering must not go too deep, and in the real world of Salford and Maggie, justice must be based on reality. Hobson is chastened, but he gets only what he is felt to have deserved – no more and no less. Justice is done, but the audience is able to enjoy the humour without it being spoilt by the arousal of a disproportionate sense of pity for Hobson.

Willie is developing as the audience knew he would. He has unexpected powers of speech and deals with Hobson beautifully, increasing his suffering by an exaggerated sympathy that moves Hobson to a frenzy and the audience to laughter. The Willie of the first act is, however, very much alive. Just as there was a reversal of role when it was Maggie and not Willie who made the proposal of marriage so here it is Willie who needs support on his wedding night. The traditional image of the eager male is transformed into a frightened little man who is terrified of being left alone with his new wife. It is the stock situation of the farcical wedding night but it remains amusing and human because it is Maggie and Willie to whom it is happening. The dimension of meaningful character is preserved, as indeed it is in the teacher/taught relationship between Maggie and Willie which operates even on this night. Here is a reversal of the Professor Higgins and Eliza Doolittle relationship that Shaw portrays in *Pygmalion*, where Higgins is teacher and master and Eliza is the wretched flower girl. Again the humour is based upon the use of symbols to make important points. The washing-up presents the same sort of symbol in this act as the wheeling of the handcart in the second. Both represent an acceptance of and a change in outlook by the character concerned; and they are a source of humour to the audience.

There is a feeling of resolution at the end of this act. This springs not only from the passing of the climax in the plot, but also from the workings of retribution on the characters. When Hobson can get near to a just appreciation of Willie Mossop, the wheel has come a full circle. Yet there have been hints that the reversal of the situation has yet far to go. The theme of class has been only gently commented on during this act. The audience will want to know more about the Mossops' future in business and in society.

gaffer Boss (Dialect).
nobbut Nothing but (Dialect).
owt Anything (Dialect).
thankless child 'How sharper than a serpent's tooth it is to have a thankless child!' (*King Lear*, I, 4, 312).
tablets of memory cf. 'Yea, from the table of my memory I'll wipe away all trivial fond records' (*Hamlet*, I, 5, 98).
outrageous fortune cf. 'Whether 'tis nobler in the mind to suffer The slings and arrows of outrageous fortune' (*Hamlet*, III, 1, 57).
Manchester Guardian Founded in 1855 it was, and is, the most important and influential paper in the North of England. It is now called *The Guardian*.
Queen Queen Victoria, the reigning monarch.
penny buns . . . tuppence A common proverbial saying about marriage.
slate Commonly used instead of paper in schools at that time.

Revision questions on Act 3

1 Show how in this act the plot begins to resolve itself.

2 In this act Maggie excels herself; she arranges not only her own life but the lives of all around her. How far is this statement correct?

3 This act could be labelled 'Hobson's downfall'. Would this be an adequate description?

4 Describe how the character and manner of Willie are changing.

Act 4

The scene is Hobson's living room. A year has passed. Jim Heeler enters. Although Hobson is ill and has sent for the doctor, he is getting up. Tubby describes, as they wait, how Hobson's affairs are going downhill. Hobson enters in a sad state of health and mind. He bemoans the way his daughters have treated him, though he agrees to Tubby's going to fetch Maggie. Hobson asserts he is dying. He has strange suicidal compulsions, the result of a lifetime's drinking habits.

Doctor MacFarlane is aggrieved to find Hobson up. When the doctor insists on seeing his patient alone, Jim leaves. The doctor bluntly tells Hobson that he is suffering from chronic alcoholism: he writes Hobson a prescription about which Hobson is rude and insulting. The doctor then tells him that he will have to give up drink completely. Hobson, who has no intention of giving it up, tries to pay the doctor's fee there and then, in order to be rid of him. Doctor MacFarlane remains, to insist that Hobson needs a woman around. He is determined to get Maggie back to take charge of her father: she is the 'cure' that Hobson needs. At this point Maggie enters.

Maggie has come because Tubby has fetched her. She now learns that her father is drinking himself to death. The doctor indicates that, though she is a married woman and though her father has treated her badly, it is her duty to live at her father's. Maggie firmly indicates that any arrangements are her business. The doctor leaves, emphasizing that Hobson's future lies in the prescription, total abstinence and Maggie.

Maggie tells Tubby to fetch Mr Mossop, whom she will have to consult about her future plans. Hobson mocks at this consultation, saying that Maggie is the dominant force in her house. At this point Alice and then Vickey arrive. Both younger daughters emphatically refuse to come to look after Hobson: Alice on the plea that she has risen in the world, and Vickey because she is expecting a baby.

When Willie Mossop arrives he is blunt about the deterioration of Hobson's shop. The sisters are uncomfortable with this self-assured Willie who treats them as equals.

When Hobson and Maggie enter, Willie's assured manner continues; he is brisk and efficient, and shows little sympathy for Hobson. Surprisingly, Hobson, hurt by his younger daughters' virtual rejection of him, tells them to leave, so that he can speak to Willie and Maggie on his own.

Hobson, his old self returning, offers Maggie and Willie a home with him on *his* conditions, which are a virtual return to the arrangements existing before they left. Willie, on hearing these proposals, rises to go. Maggie tells Willie to state his conditions. Maggie is proud of him and he is proud of her. Maggie asks to be consulted over any improvements. Willie tries to remove the brass wedding ring in order to get a better one. Maggie refuses. She will wear a gold ring for show, but the brass one stays, a reminder to them of what they really are, no matter how successful they become. A meek Hobson returns, wearing his hat, then leaves with Maggie. A triumphant, amazed Willie remains for a moment. His disbelief, surprise and happiness are all summed up in his 'Well, by gum!'

Commentary

This final act amplifies the threads in the plot at the end of Act 3. Hobson's punishment has continued, inflicted not by others but by himself. Drink to which he was always disposed has now taken him over completely. The crux comes when he is visited by Dr MacFarlane, a Scottish doctor who is as outspoken and blunt as Hobson himself. His professional bluntness emphasizes the sorry state to which Hobson has come. In this world of comedy it must be resolved. Maggie, together with Willie, is the resolution. Yet this time it is Willie who is triumphant not Maggie. The act represents not only the salvation of Hobson, his acceptance of reality, the revelation of the uselessness of his bluster, his false pride, and his illusions; it also shows the completion of the growth of Willie's character. He has become a man. His marriage to Maggie is a partnership in the fullest sense.

Perhaps Willie may ultimately become the more dominant character. Hobson is certainly no match for him in cunning, in understanding or in striking a bargain.

Alice and Vickey are shown to be basically the shallow, selfish characters they had appeared in previous acts. In them there is no benevolence and little humanity. Their houses, their social status and their futures are more important to them than their father. They do not make excuses; in their world and with their scale of values these refusals represent genuine reasons, not excuses, for opting out of their duty to their father. Self-interest is their motivating force.

The act underlines what was predicted at the end of the previous act. Mossop's is now more successful than Hobson's. This is a reversal of situation. Hobson's is not the end of the road. Willie is set to attain a success that Hobson never could. If there is a moral here, and perhaps in a comedy set in Victorian Salford this would not be out of place, it is that success comes to those who are genuinely prepared to work for it, who have an honest knowledge of themselves, and who possess a just estimation of their own worth and the service they can give to others. Willie has developed these and that is why the audience is left feeling that Hobson's is only a stage in Willie's future success.

The humour has been less evident in this act. Hobson's alcoholism and the daughters' selfishness and hardness have added touches that suggest a darker side. In the end all is resolved, but the audience on the way has had a glimpse or two of a harsh reality. Everyone gets what they deserve out of life, and there is a pleasant sense of completeness. There are no loose ends in the plot. The different characters have been carefully allocated to their proper positions. Justice has been done, but not too harshly. Lessons have been learned, but not too painfully. The final act, although different in tone from the others, is still firmly set in the world of comedy, and, according to their deserts, the different characters will live happily ever after.

Prince Consort Prince Albert (1819–61): married to Queen Victoria.
Lord Beaconsfield Benjamin Disraeli (1804–81), statesman and novelist; he was several times Prime Minister.
Antimacassars An ornamental covering over the back of a chair.
a cut line An unprofitable one.
Young woman with her first i.e. first child.
ken Know (Dialect, Scottish).
foreigner Here a Scotsman, Doctor MacFarlane.
Chronic alcoholism Serious illness brought on by too much consumption of alcohol.
body Person (Dialect).
shut of Rid of.
Crescent One of the few remaining examples of Georgian architecture in Salford.
worrits Worries (Dialect).
cedars of Lebanon There are many references to these in the Old Testament.
owt Anything (Dialect).

Revision questions on Act 4

1 *Hobson's Choice*, like all good comedy, leaves the audience in a warm glow of happiness and satisfaction at the end. How far is this statement correct?

2 There are signs in Act 4 that Willie will be at least level with Maggie in the future. What signs point to this conclusion?

3 Vickey and Alice turn out to be poor creatures, and Hobson recognizes this. Discuss.

4 Attempt a brief sketch, in either narrative or dramatic form, of a possible fifth act showing what happens when Willie, Maggie and Hobson are together.

Harold Brighouse's art in *Hobson's Choice*

Style

Comedy stems mainly from character, situation and dialogue; its purpose is to amuse, and in this the play succeeds splendidly. It is rich in the many forms of humour that are most effective in the theatre.

'In play-writing,' Brighouse wrote, 'I put character first.' The humorous aspect of the characters is the most enduring source of comedy in the play. They are largely stock types, easily recognizable by the audience; there is, in broad conception, nothing very striking or original about any of them. Hobson himself is the portrayal of a conventional type of stage northerner: a good deal of bluster, outspokenness verging on rudeness, and a close regard for money. Hobson is, of course, much more than this, though the basic stage type is there. Similarly, in the other characters basic types can be traced in the two daughters, provincial snobbery bent on swift marriage; the change from mouse to man in Willie Mossop; the irascible Scottish doctor; the overbearing, wealthy old woman.

The minor characters come near to caricature but the more important ones take on individual traits; though, it must be admitted, it is a little difficult to distinguish between the characters of Alice and Vickey. The play could have gained interest had they been more clearly differentiated. Nevertheless, they are there primarily to amuse us, not to provide an insight into the depth or variety of human foibles. The portrayal of the minor characters – both in themselves and in their relationships with each other – is richly comic. Place Willie against Hobson and the audience recognizes a sure formula for amusement; as is the juxtaposition of Maggie with her sisters, their two young men, or Ada Figgins.

It is not possible to divide character completely from situation. Incidents are amusing in *Hobson's Choice* not so much because they are funny in themselves but because of the men and women who take part in them – for instance, Maggie's taking Willie by the ear to lead him into the bedroom on their wedding night. The wedding night episode gains immeasurably in humour because of the peculiar background to the relationship of Willie and Maggie and because of their individual character traits. Hobson's visit to Maggie's home on the night of the wedding is full of potentially hilarious situations: again we laugh because of our interest in Hobson's character.

There is very little suggestion of true farce in the play: situations are seldom important in themselves. Not only do they reveal, and gain from, character differences; they are also an organic part of the total plot. The humour is on two levels: the laughter of the audience is aroused but the interest in what is going to happen is also maintained. There is a certain comic irony in Hobson's appealing to Maggie when he thinks an action for damages against him is imminent; in terms of the progression of the narrative it is also essential that the result should be in accordance with Maggie's plan.

The third main source of humour is that of dialogue, or the wit of individual speeches; in this the play abounds. The characters as they express their attitudes, ideas and prejudices provide a fund of northern down-to-earth wit. It is not always original. Indeed, part of the humour sometimes lies in the use of a commonplace, proverbial saying. 'Your penny buns 'll cost you tuppence now' is still effective though it is not original: it fits the character and the mood of disillusionment that overwhelms Hobson at that time. He has an oratorical turn of phrase. At times he can be pungent and witty: 'Honest men live by business and lawyers live by law'; 'There's a difference between affording and paying'; 'Life's got to be worth living before I'll live it'. Such aphoristic statements reveal the accomplishment and the wit of the style.

Background and style are inextricably linked. *Hobson's Choice*, like so many of the naturalistic plays produced by the Manchester School, belongs in style and feeling to the industrial North, reflecting in particular the predominantly harsh world of Salford in the 1880s. It is no environment of polish or culture; common sense, wit proceeding from experience, and simple language are the salient qualities. There is no room for width of cultural reference or sophisticated, epigrammatic conversation; imagination and vividness of expression exist, but there are no flights of fancy. Art is represented by portraits, on the walls of Hobson's living room, of the Prince Consort, Queen Victoria and the Earl of Beaconsfield. The audience never learns which book Vickey is reading – the fact that she is reading at all indicates her pretensions rather than her intelligence.

The style has only the appearance, not the reality, of roughness: the characters are capable of turning nicely balanced and effective sentences; even the doctor is skilled in this balance: 'One prescription is on the table, Mrs Mossop. The other two are total abstinence and – you.' Dramatically, this is simple, telling and perfectly phrased, though there is nothing in what is said but practical everyday ideas.

Generally sentences are short, though Hobson can at times rise to a grand climax of sentence construction. Dialogue is often simple:

Willie: Come home, Maggie.
Maggie: I think I'll have to.
Hobson: Whatever's the hurry for? (Act 4, p.78)

Three brief speeches yet, in their simplicity, they express effectively a significant moment in the resolution of the plot and the relationship of the three characters. Devices of language are used sparingly; there is the alliteration of 'Pampering pays', which emphasizes the force of the worldly Northern wisdom. The analogies are obvious:

Jim: You've to bait your hook to catch fish, Henry.
Hobson: Then, I'll none go fishing.

The images themselves are from the world of everyday objects: 'Your daughter's not the sort to want the truth wrapped round with a feather-bed for fear it hurts her hand' (Act 4, p.69). Weddings going through a family 'like measles' provides a simple but graphic simile.

Much of the atmosphere of *Hobson's Choice* lies in its use of dialect, though Brighouse wisely decided not to employ dialect to such an extent that it became a stumbling-block to a non-Lancastrian audience. It is seldom used to distinguish one character from another; Hobson's dialect is as broad as that of his two workmen, and we must remember that he prides himself on being middle class. It was, of course, a mark of Northern society that all classes tended to speak with an accent, however slight. There are, of course, degrees: plainly Albert's legal studies have left their mark on his own use of English, which is relatively standard.

Most of the dialect words are obvious in meaning. *None* is used for 'not' ('I'm *none* in love with you', 'You'll *none* rule me'); *owt* for 'anything'; *them* for 'these'; *road* for 'way'; *nay* for 'no'; *aye* for 'yes'; *worrits* for 'worries'; *diddled* for 'trusted'; *warm* for 'well-off'. Archaic words survive: *gotten* for 'got'; *dost, you's*.

The article is frequently omitted and sometimes part of the word: *'ud, 'em, your feet on pavement, open door*. There is reversion of word order (*They're Willies making, those*). The double negative is used for emphasis (*no use to nobody*). There are characteristic phrases: *nobbut one, us two, our Maggie, by gum*.

The characters

Henry Horatio Hobson

Hobson is a man of fifty-five, successful, insensitive, self-important, and noisy. His main pleasure in life is talking and drinking at the Moonraker's Inn. He likes his drink, but he has never drunk to excess until Maggie leaves him. His friend Jim regards him as an orator. The full force of his oratory can be seen when he endeavours to put his daughters in their place in the first act. At times his sentences can rise to a nice antithetical balance: 'I stand for common-sense and sincerity. You're affected, which is bad sense and insincerity' (p.6). At times his talk has the eloquence and style of the great periods of oratory (see p.7). At its best his speech combines passionate conviction with powerful expression. Sometimes the subject is unworthy of the eloquence, but that is the comedy. 'I've had my liquor for as long as I remember, and I'll have it to the end. If I'm to be beaten by beer I'll die fighting, and I'm none practising unnatural teetotalism for the sake of lengthening out my unalcoholic days. Life's got to be worth living before I'll live it' (Act 4, p.66).

Alas, no one outside the Moonraker's parlour – and we never witness what happens there – takes much notice of his flowers of oratory. He admits himself that in the eyes of his daughters he is a 'windbag'. His eloquence has little effect on Doctor MacFarlane, and even young Albert Prosser can cope with it. The truth is, as Jim points out to him, 'Roaring is mainly hollow sound . . . it's steel in a man's character that subdues the women' (Act 1, p.12), and it is just this steel that Hobson so manifestly lacks. It is little wonder that his daughters have no respect for him when they witness performances like the one with Mrs Hepworth, where he combines obsequiousness and a total lack of pride with a foolish and unconvincing attempt to re-establish himself when she has gone.

Hobson is a bully and, like many of his kind, is weak and cowardly. When he hears that Maggie is to marry Willie, he attempts to give Willie a leathering; Willie stands up for himself manfully, and Hobson is at a loss to know what to do next. By the same token, at the end of the play, when Hobson's proposals for the future are decisively rejected he gives in virtually without a struggle, and follows Maggie meekly, obediently, like a dog at heel.

Hobson has all the narrow prejudices of the Victorian lower-middle-class Englishman: he never tires of boasting that he is British middle class (he should say 'English', for he regards the Scottish doctor as a foreigner). He takes a strong pride in his roots – it is 'Salford lads' who are the cream of Englishmen. He believes strongly that man is the master of woman – incapable though he is of translating this belief into practice – and admits that even his own daughters have the upper hand of him. His relief when (before the play opens) his wife had died suggests that he had been equally dominated in marriage (Act 1, p.12).

Hobson detests both doctors and lawyers, yet his behaviour lands him in the hands of both.

There is little moral sense in Hobson. Respectability is his religion, being a vicar's warden at St Philip's its ultimate expression. Were he not so foolish he would be a worldly-wise man, for he knows that respectability is good for business.

His tastes are conservative. The furniture in his living room is that of the conventional lower-middle-class family of the time; the room is overcrowded, with an abundance of anti-macassars and portraits of royalty and the prime minister. He objects violently to his daughters following the fashion in clothes. His description of the bustle is a comic delight (Act 1, p.6).

Despite his expansive manner, Hobson is mean. The prospect of paying damages is repellent to him; procuring a settlement for his daughters' marriages is like extracting a tooth. Mrs Hepworth is quite right when she takes it for granted that he is underpaying Willie: not only does he pay him a pittance at the beginning, he also, with magnificent impudence, proposes that Willie shall revert to his former wage when, at the end, he returns to Hobson's. His extrovert manner gives the appearance of generosity, but only Hobson himself is deceived by it. He is strongly opposed to the idea of Maggie's ever getting married: she is far too useful to part with.

He is, however, capable of inspiring loyalty, and sometimes even liking. Willie was content in his own way before Maggie decided to marry him; Tubby is loyal, against his own interests; Doctor MacFarlane, though seeing him at his worst, feels kindly towards him.

Pride is all to him: 'I'm Hobson,' he declares, as if that explains everything. He could be saying 'I'm Napoleon', or 'I'm the Duke of Wellington'. It is both comic and pathetic that he is driven to the most pitiful subterfuges to bolster his pride, both to others and to himself. 'I'm going to put a collar on,' he responds to Maggie's insistence, 'But understand me, Maggie, it's not for the sake of Will Mossop. It's because my neck is cold' (Act 4, p.73). Vickey and Alice can play cleverly on this, suggesting a way out for Hobson at such awkward moments. However, they are not always successful: when Vickey argues that he is not being beaten by a lawyer because instead of having to pay a thousand pounds he need only pay five hundred, he is hardly convinced. 'I'd take a good few beatings myself at the price,' he remarks ruefully.

Hobson finally sees through the selfishness of Vickey and Alice in the last scene: it is difficult to understand why it has taken him so long. Having done so, he is blunt to the point of brutality (Act 4, p.77).

Hobson's fundamental weakness of character is in his tendency to self-pity and his turning to drink for consolation. He has reached the stage of chronic alcoholism when he is terrified of drowning when he is washing, and of deliberately cutting his throat when he handles his razor. He blames his heavy drinking on Maggie, and suggests, in an attempt to arouse her pity, that it is because she is an ungrateful child.

Despite her authoritarian approach, Maggie obviously cares for him. Willie is worried about Hobson's state because it worries Maggie. No doubt Hobson will be reasonably content with Maggie and Willie; he will have the illusion of power and the reality of security without the burden of responsibility. Maggie will make him toe the line and this will give him something to grumble about at the Moonraker's – if he is allowed to go there. For a man so wholly selfish, mean, hypocritical and weak, it is not a bad fate. In one sense the play is about his downfall; this, however, is a comedy and the ending is happy enough.

Maggie Hobson

In terms of plot, Maggie is the pivot. Yet she is relatively simply drawn: thirty years of age, determined, efficient and a born organizer. She likes to give the impression of being completely unsentimental. Yet she cannot entirely smother the sentiment in her – witness her taking a flower to press in her Bible as a keepsake of her wedding day. At the end of the play sentiment mellows into true philosophy: 'I'll wear your gold for show, but that brass stays where you put it, Will, and if we get too rich and proud we'll just sit down together quiet and take a long look at it, so as we'll not forget the truth about ourselves' (Act 4, p.82). For all its strange beginnings, Maggie's marriage to Will will be a good one. The final 'Eh, lad!' and 'Eh, lass!' express deep affection.

Maggie is an organizer of other people's lives, sometimes just good-heartedly, but more often to ensure that her plans work out successfully. It is a fine piece of altruism that she engineers her sisters' marriages: she owes them nothing and will get no thanks for achieving it; but there is a generosity of disposition and a sense of fairness that drive her on. In this she is quite unlike her sisters and her father: it would never occur to Maggie to brood on who was going to benefit from Hobson's will.

Her independence can be tempered with tact and Mrs Hepworth certainly approved of her.

Albert sees the dangers of Maggie's domination and worries that if they give in to her now they will be under her thumb for the rest of their lives. But he is sufficiently shrewd to recognize that Maggie is working in his best interests – more effectively than he can himself. He is, however, still taken aback when she is not surprised to find him doing the washing-up, because, as she says, she told him to!

Maggie will make a better wife than her sisters. She is, however, determined from the beginning to establish the right framework wherein the man is in charge, and works untiringly towards preparing Willie for that position. To hand over the reins to Willie prematurely would be a disaster, as she knows perfectly well. As Willie, under her guidance and encouragement, gains in confidence, education and authority he will begin to take over – with Maggie's full agreement and support. The process is substantially under way by the end of the play.

Maggie is no visionary idealist. True to her kind, she believes that success lies in money. Initially she may live in two cellars, with cast-off furniture, but that is far from her aim in life. She marries Willie, not because she sees him as a failure and a man who needs help, but because she recognizes in him a tremendous potential for success. Her sisters care only for appearances: what concerns Maggie is the *substance* of success. She even relishes the lowly beginning, because the eventual success will seem the greater (Act 2, p.34). Maggie has an abundance of pride, with nothing false about it. She never argues: she orders and she states: contradiction is impossible. When Hobson objects to being told that dinner is at one she merely goes on repeating it.

Despite her obvious strength, Maggie as a character is not entirely convincing. She is too unerringly right, too independent and too forceful; yet the hearts of the audience warm to her. Being a comedy, the authority, because it is well meant, is amusing. In real life Maggie would be an intolerable woman, with whom we would, like Willie, dread to be left alone. Here, because of her honesty and goodness, we accept and like her. She serves to highlight the foibles and the humour of the other characters and, though not funny in herself, is the cause of our laughter at them.

Willie Mossop

Willie Mossop is the one character in *Hobson's Choice* who develops during the course of the play. Hobson may, at the end, be a wiser man, but fundamentally he has not changed.

When we first see Willie, aged thirty, thin, badly clothed and uneducated, his appearance is like that of 'a rabbit' as Mrs Hepworth remarks. He is an excellent bootmaker but appears a poor specimen of a human being. He has his standards and he is loyal to Hobson's.

Even at the beginning he can – to an extent – stand up for himself. His approach is conventional, and he regards being in love as a necessary preliminary to marriage: he is not in love with Maggie, as he tells her candidly. Willie's manhood has been flattered by Ada's dependence on him; but there is about him an unselfconscious lack of pride.

In a general way Hobson approves of him, though that certainly does not extend to him as one of the family. Even at the end, when Hobson has swallowed so much, he is still Will Mossop his former workman. Hobson's sympathy keeps returning, however: 'Take you for all in all, you're the best of the bunch. You're a backward lad, but you know your trade and it's an honest one' (Act 3, p.55). Ironically, it is Willie whom he asks to open the door for Alice and Vickey to show them out (Act 4, p.77).

By the end of the first act the transformation of Willie has started. As the play develops he becomes not only more sure of himself, but more human. When Alice kisses him, he observes, 'There's more in kissing nice young women than I thought'.

Willie's modesty can be a source of strength. He is able to apologize to Hobson for not being much good at talking, and always saying the wrong thing – in his simplicity, he has upset Hobson more by stating the obvious about the dangers of publicity than he could have done by the most calculating viciousness. He is convinced he is a poor speaker, yet Alice is sure that the fluent and accomplished Albert will speak less effectively at the wedding party than Willie has done (Act 3, p.40).

Willie's wedding night is uproarious comedy; his unwillingness to be left alone with Maggie is a source of amusement to those two socially confident young men, Albert and Freddie. He has fitfully advanced in assurance, in this scene; yet when Maggie comes to him, takes him by the ear and leads him into the bedroom, there is a feeling that the development of his character has been sacrificed for the sake of the laughter that his undignified situation arouses. It makes little difference. The real and consistent transformation is to come in Act 4.

No one believes in the change. Hobson, Alice and Vickey all insist that Maggie wears the trousers. She does not deny this, simply pointing out that 'My husband's my husband', implying that this is the role that from now on Willie has to play. And he does: he begins by ordering Maggie to go and bring her father (Act 4, p.75). Swiftly and effectively he puts Vickey and Alice in their places (p.75). He reminds them that it was he and Maggie who made her sisters' marriages possible. He is fearlessly blunt with Hobson: 'There used to be room for improvement,' he replies to Hobson's statement that he is a changed man (p.76).

Willie is no fool and objects to Hobson's treating him as one in the proposals he makes. Finally it is Willie who lays down the conditions, except in the matter of the name of 'William Mossop, late Hobson', where he has still to compromise with Maggie. Otherwise he is extravagantly and completely triumphant. The 'rabbit' has become 'Master of Hobson's'. It is Maggie's doing, but she is proud of him. Success in business and in marriage is clearly to be his: this is but the beginning.

Alice Hobson

Alice is twenty-three, two years older than Vickey and seven years younger than Maggie. She is fond of having her own way but, like everyone else, is no match for Maggie. She is, for example, unable to prevent Maggie's hinting that Albert spends too much time in the shop by dictatorially selling him a pair of boots he does not want. Alice can, nevertheless, argue her point with her sister, unkindly calling her an 'old maid' in the process. Hobson cuts no ice with her when he objects to the way she dresses. She at once asserts her independence and her desire to be abreast of fashion.

Snobbery is a major part of Alice's character. The opinion of Sam Minns does not count because he is a publican; and she is scandalized by Maggie's proposed marriage to Willie Mossop. Later she is puffed up with pride at being Mrs Albert Prosser and of living in the Crescent; 'cast-off furniture' is not for her.

Alice is extraordinarily inefficient in the shop; she is quite incapable of giving the simplest instructions to Tubby and keeping the accounts is beyond her. In truth, she is totally uninterested in the family business, but needle-sharp where her own affairs are concerned. When Maggie is collecting old furniture from the attic, Alice is very much alive to her own future claims. She is more than willing for Maggie to look after Hobson, but she can, at Vickey's prompting, see the danger of being left out of her father's will.

Alice's real interest is in getting married, because she sees in marriage to Albert Prosser a release from the tedium of working in the shop and the establishment of herself in a state of society and a way of life that she covets. She is singularly ungrateful to Maggie for making this possible. She and Albert will suit each other, but he will not have things all his own way. Even before they are married, she can silence him very effectively: 'Sit down. We've had enough of speeches. I know men fancy themselves when they're talking, but you've had one turn and you needn't start again.' Just as in Shakespeare's *Taming of the Shrew* it is Katharina who proves finally to be an obedient wife and Bianca, her younger sister, who asserts her independence in marriage, so it may well be here with Maggie and Alice.

Victoria Hobson

Hobson's youngest daughter, Vickey, is the prettiest yet the most colourless of the three. Reading is her chief occupation, enabling her to remove herself from the world around her. She gives a little scream when Maggie flings the boot box at her while she is immersed in her book. She can, however, be independent and is obviously Hobson's favourite.

She sympathizes with Alice, but she does not really care about others or their troubles. When Alice wonders whether she has done the right thing in instructing Tubby to make clogs, she is not in the least concerned about the likely outcome, as the blame can be laid at her father's door (Act 2, p.27). But her understanding stops when she is brought into it herself: 'You needn't be snappy with me about it.' Like Alice, she sees in marriage a means of escape, and the sum of all her ambitions; but she has been less blatant in her pursuit of Freddy Beenstock than has Alice in hers of Albert.

Vickey clearly has a reputation for quiet cunning and, perhaps, dishonesty. Witness her father's comment in Act 1 (p.5).

When Hobson is ill, Vickey is the most outwardly affectionate of the three sisters. It means little. Her inbuilt egocentricity and selfishness are such that she is quite genuinely puzzled that she should be expected to put herself out in any way to help. She is hypocritically sentimental when she insists that her child comes first – it is Vickey who does!

Like Alice she is plainly showing a measure of independence towards her husband: 'If Alice and I don't need to ask our husbands, I'm sure you never need ask yours,' she says impatiently to Maggie.

She can be blunt, but it is youthful tactlessness rather than an ingrained character trait.

Vickey's cunning is evident when she alerts Alice to the danger of allowing Maggie to live with Hobson, in the light of what he might leave (and to whom) in his will. She still feels proprietorial rights in the shop, even though she is glad to be out of it and has no intentions of helping in any way. If we were comparing Hobson's three daughters with those of Lear, it is to Regan, the spiteful and cunning, that we should liken Vickey.

Albert Prosser

Albert is an up-and-coming young man. He is twenty-six and the son of a solicitor, looks after his clothes and grooms his hair. He knows what he wants, is fairly sure of himself, and will doubtless achieve much in life. He is no match for Maggie to whom he can offer no opposition when she is determined to sell him a pair of boots against his will. Maggie is tired of his young-man-in-love act, and his frequent presence in the shop in order to court Alice (Act 1, p.4).

He is a competent lawyer, however, pronouncing with some authority that the action he has made out on Maggie's instructions may not be good law.

He has, not surprisingly, some of Freddy's sense of social convention. The idea of pushing a hand-cart through Salford appals him. He is profoundly disturbed by the possibility that some of his friends may see him. But he does push the hand-cart when urged to by the formidable Maggie.

There is a lively sense of self-interest in Albert. He is prepared to remain in Maggie's good books while she can be useful to him, though he points out shrewdly that if they give in to her now, she will dominate them for the rest of their days.

Like Freddie, Albert feels much consternation at the arrival of Hobson. When, however, he has as a lawyer to confront Hobson, he does very well indeed. He rides Hobson's insulting comments about lawyers (Act 3, p.52), and gets down to business. He can even turn the tables on Hobson's insults by reminding him that they could be added to his legal costs.

When he asks for a thousand pounds, Maggie comments that she can see he is going to get on in the world. He may be a match for Hobson, but is quite incapable of standing up to Maggie. It is Albert who, after seeing the success of Willie's and Maggie's efforts to launch a business, immediately enquires where they raised the capital.

Albert likes to talk, and it is only with difficulty that Alice restrains him from making a speech in reply to Willie's at the wedding celebration. He and Alice will make a good pair. They are both alive to their own advantage, and Alice has enough spirit to be a match for him. Their social and financial ambitions are identical, making them ideal inhabitants of the exclusive Crescent.

Fred Beenstock

He is the respectable son of a respectable man of business – Jonathan Beenstock and Co, Corn Merchants of Chapel Street, Salford – in the same street as Hobson's Boot Shop. He is an attractive young man, not a dandy, but good-looking enough to attract Vickey. He has tact and delicacy. He does not tell Vickey that her father fell into the cellar because he was too drunk to see but fabricates a more acceptable story.

At first, he willingly submits to Maggie's ordering-about: he gets out one word of objection when she asks him to help with the sofa, but that is all. When he is asked to wash pots his objections are more vocal; but in the end he does help with the washing-up, even though Maggie is not there.

Freddy has a degree of social assurance; he is amused at the idea of Willie's being scared of being left alone with his wife. It is something he could not imagine happening to himself – though on his perform-ance with Maggie he might well not measure up much better than Willie does. Freddy is plainly a very conventional young man in thought and conduct, and it is the unusualness of Willie's position that amuses and puzzles him. Washing-up is for him an unusual occupation; that is why he expects Maggie to show gratitude to him for doing it. To his conventional mind the idea of Vickey and Alice living at home after the quarrel with Hobson seems impossible. He will obviously be the amiable and well-to-do husband Vickey demands. He is portrayed as having little personality: his impact on the audience is limited; and he is overshadowed, even in his minor part, by Albert.

Mrs Hepworth

Mrs Hepworth has three main functions in the play: the first is to reveal Hobson's fundamental weakness, and his ingratiating obsequiousness; the second is to emphasize the quality of Willie Mossop's workmanship and, incidentally, to introduce him to us; the third is to provide comedy by Mrs Hepworth's own curt imperiousness.

She is a well-dressed old lady, brusque in manner. She treats everyone as a servant. However she makes small distinction in her treatment of people; we suspect that she treats high and low in the same imperious manner. She is plainly a shrewd and impartial judge of character, for she decides that Willie is 'a treasure'. Hobson she plainly regards as a skinflint.

Mrs Hepworth provides a lot of fun while she is on stage. We enjoy her and wish she had stayed longer.

Timothy Wadlow

Tubby is a small white-haired man, with thin legs, a paunch, and poor clothes. He knows his work. It is he who has taught Willie bootmaking. He lacks initiative: though he is the foreman he has to be told what to do, even if by a woman who knows little about the business – he needs his orders. But he has his pride as a craftsman: in his opinion a foreman shoehand should not be doing domestic work. He is loyal, even to a man like Hobson, and sticks to him – even though everyone calls Tubby a fool for not putting his own interests first. He is no fool, however: he knows exactly what is the state of things at Hobson's. He is a good judge of character, as he shows in his accurate summing-up of Maggie, Willie and Hobson. He will doubtless accept easily and be very happy under Willie's management.

Jim Heeler

He is a grocer, and Hobson's drinking companion. It is to him that Hobson goes with his troubles. Jim has a lively admiration for Hobson, especially for his oratory. His horizons are, of course, limited to the parlour of the Moonraker's.

Like Hobson he has a gift for a strong turn of phrase. He is not without his own load of down-to-earth wisdom and perspicuity. 'And it's steel in a man's character that subdues the woman,' he says, (Act 1, p.12), putting his finger unerringly on Hobson's weakness. He is more knowledgeable than Hobson; it is he who points out the realities of marriage settlements.

He has a sense of propriety – as when he tells Tubby he ought not to be discussing Hobson's business secrets with him. He is cautiously optimistic in dealing with the sick Hobson; but he loses to Doctor MacFarlane. We feel that he is a sounder man than Hobson and would be better at standing up for himself.

Ada Figgins

Ada is Maggie's opposite in personality. She is weak, fair-haired, pale and lacking in vitality. Her age is twenty; she dresses in clogs and shawl, typical wear for girls of her class at that time.

She brings Willie's dinner in at the time when Maggie has been discussing marriage with him. Willie has stated that he is spoken for. According to Maggie, a marriage to Ada would be a disaster for Willie. He would remain a slave, even if a contented one – an eighteen shilling-a-week bootmaker all his life. Ada would make nothing of him.

Ada is no match for Maggie, who endeavours to soften the blow by telling her that Willie is not much for them to quarrel over. Ada has her loyalty; and she praises Willie's playing of the Jew's harp. She is also simply sentimental: 'I see the lad I love,' she says without any embarrassment.

Ada is soon routed and falls back on the hope that her mother will be able to put matters right. Plainly Mrs Figgins is a more fearsome woman than her daughter: Willie is afraid of her tongue; he is joyful when he discovers that he need go back there no more.

Ada is treated outrageously, but we care little: we are too interested in Maggie at this moment in the play. Ada is not really a figure of pathos: she does not fight enough to command sympathy; and her final hope that her mother will sort things out merely evokes our scorn. We are relieved that Willie has escaped the clutches of Mrs Figgins, if not Ada's.

Doctor MacFarlane

Hobson as an invalid is a difficult man to handle; Doctor MacFarlane, a Scottish doctor aged fifty – who speaks with a Scots accent, and frequently in the dialect – copes with him superbly. He begins by attacking Hobson for being well enough to be out of bed and downstairs, pointing out that he himself has been up all night delivering a baby. He then drives out Jim Heeler.

Hobson intends to master the doctor but the doctor very quickly masters him – despite Hobson's general hostility to doctors and medicine (which almost equals his hatred of lawyers and the law).

The doctor is every bit as blunt as Hobson. He neither ignores nor accepts Hobson's rudeness and is dictatorial with him (Act 4, p.66). He tells Hobson not what he ought to do but what he will do.

Hobson would indeed be glad to get rid of him, and in his desire to do so is even very anxious to pay him on the spot. However, the doctor now is moving into a position of dominance. He regards Hobson as a 'pig-headed animal': he tells him that he will die sober. He lectures him on the value of women, and orders him to get Maggie back.

Maggie arrives, and the doctor is now certain that Hobson will be saved. He is a shrewd judge of character: he was right in thinking that Maggie was the name of the cure Hobson needed.

This is a play with an astonishingly high proportion of blunt characters. Doctor MacFarlane shows that the blunt Scot is at least the equal of the blunt Lancastrian.

General questions

1 The audience sees the world of *Hobson's Choice* chiefly through the eyes of Maggie. Comment on this statement.

Points to cover in your answer

The leading character in terms of the impact made on the audience. Plot revolves around her in relationships and movement. All schemes (e.g. to get Hobson to agree to the marriages of Alice and Vickey, to instil ambition in Willie Mossop, to effect her own marriage) are hatched and carried to a successful conclusion by Maggie.

Consider how far the audience identify with her through her energy, her wit, her common sense.

Would her unconventional ideas be a stumbling block to a contemporary audience? Would the reversal of roles in her early relationship with Willie be objected to by some? How does a modern audience view this aspect?

How far would her dominating character offend some of the audience? The more conventional men in the contemporary audience, the Hobsons of the world, for example.

Is the audience prepared to see other characters through her eyes and to accept her judgements of them? Is there some sympathy for other characters that lessens the identification with Maggie e.g. for Hobson or Albert?

Examine whether Willie Mossop attracts the sympathy of the audience as well as, more than or less than Maggie.

Estimate to what extent the audience has a genuine affection for Maggie – or a dislike. With reference to the text show how attitudes to her may differ at various points in the play: this is connected with the degree of development in her character which is slight compared to that of Willie Mossop.

Look at her part in the various themes of the play e.g. class, the Victorian gospel of getting on in business and social life, family relationships.

2 For a play in a Victorian setting, *Hobson's Choice* gives a very unusual view of women. State in what respects this view *is* unusual, and say how far the statement is correct.

3 Humour springs from both character and situation. How far is this true of *Hobson's Choice*?

4 Maggie is not only the strongest character in *Hobson's Choice*; she also controls the workings of the plot. Discuss.

5 Examine the extent to which Brighouse reproduces the flavour of local speech in the play. Consider how far this would be an obstacle to, say, a London audience.

6 Describe the changes that take place in Hobson's position during the course of the play.

7 Harold Brighouse is adept at sketching effective minor characters. Amplify this statement by reference to Mrs Hepworth, Ada Figgins and Doctor MacFarlane.

8 Outline the development in the character of Willie Mossop during the play.

9 The world of *Hobson's Choice* is a small one, preoccupied with social standing and the making of money. Discuss.

10 Brighouse excels in the creation of vivid dialogue, appropriate to the character speaking and expressive of the Northern background. Discuss.

11 On the whole the world of *Hobson's Choice* is a kindly one, where human beings have amusing weaknesses but nothing vicious about them. Discuss.

12 *Hobson's Choice* is a satire on middle-class respectability. How far is this true?

13 What view of marriage is given in *Hobson's Choice*?

14 How far does the unfolding and resolution of the plot maintain the interest of the audience?

15 Who is the most important male character in *Hobson's Choice*?

16 Which scene in *Hobson's Choice* is the most humorous? Describe the scene and analyse its appeal.

Further reading

Oscar Wilde *The Importance of Being Earnest*
Stanley Houghton *Hindle Wakes*
George Bernard Shaw *Pygmalion*

Pan study aids Titles published in the Brodie's Notes series

W. H. Auden Selected Poetry

Jane Austen Emma Mansfield Park Northanger Abbey Persuasion
Pride and Prejudice

Anthologies of Poetry Ten Twentieth Century Poets
The Poet's Tale The Metaphysical Poets

Samuel Beckett Waiting for Godot

Arnold Bennett The Old Wives' Tale

William Blake Songs of Innocence and Experience

Robert Bolt A Man for All Seasons

Charlotte Brontë Jane Eyre

Emily Brontë Wuthering Heights

Robert Browning Selected Poetry

John Bunyan The Pilgrim's Progress

Geoffrey Chaucer (parallel texts editions) The Franklin's Tale
The Knight's Tale The Miller's Tale The Nun's Priest's Tale
The Pardoner's Tale Prologue to the Canterbury Tales
The Wife of Bath's Tale

John Clare Selected Poetry and Prose

Wilkie Collins The Woman in White

William Congreve The Way of the World

Joseph Conrad Heart of Darkness
The Nigger of the Narcissus Youth The Secret Agent

Charles Dickens Dombey and Son Hard Times Little Dorrit
Oliver Twist Our Mutual Friend A Tale of Two Cities

Gerald Durrell My Family and Other Animals

George Eliot Middlemarch The Mill on the Floss Silas Marner

T. S. Eliot Murder in the Cathedral Selected Poems

J. G. Farrell The Siege of Krishnapur

William Faulkner As I Lay Dying

Henry Fielding Joseph Andrews

F. Scott Fitzgerald The Great Gatsby

E. M. Forster Howards End A Passage to India
Where Angels Fear to Tread

Elizabeth Gaskell North and South

William Golding Lord of the Flies The Spire

Oliver Goldsmith She Stoops to Conquer

Graham Greene Brighton Rock The Power and the Glory
The Quiet American The Human Factor

Thomas Hardy Chosen Poems of Thomas Hardy
Far from the Madding Crowd Jude the Obscure
The Mayor of Casterbridge Return of the Native Tess of the d'Urbervilles
The Trumpet-Major

L. P. Hartley The Go-Between The Shrimp and the Anemone

Joseph Heller Catch-22

Ernest Hemingway A Farewell to Arms For Whom the Bell Tolls
The Old Man and the Sea

Barry Hines A Kestrel for a Knave

Henry James Washington Square

Ben Jonson The Alchemist Volpone

James Joyce A Portrait of the Artist as a Young Man Dubliners

John Keats Selected Poems and Letters of John Keats

Ken Kesey One Flew over the Cuckoo's Nest

Rudyard Kipling Kim

D. H. Lawrence The Rainbow Selected Tales Sons and Lovers

Harper Lee To Kill a Mockingbird

Laurie Lee As I Walked out One Midsummer Morning Cider with Rosie

Christopher Marlowe Doctor Faustus Edward the Second

W. Somerset Maugham Of Human Bondage

Gavin Maxwell Ring of Bright Water

Thomas Middleton The Changeling

Arthur Miller The Crucible Death of a Salesman

John Milton A Choice of Milton's Verse Comus and Samson
Agonistes Paradise Lost I, II

Sean O'Casey Juno and the Paycock
The Shadow of a Gunman and the Plough and the Stars

George Orwell Animal Farm 1984

John Osborne Luther

Alexander Pope Selected Poetry

J. B. Priestley An Inspector Calls

J. D. Salinger The Catcher in the Rye

Siegfried Sassoon Memoirs of a Fox-Hunting Man

Peter Shaffer The Royal Hunt of the Sun

William Shakespeare Antony and Cleopatra
As You Like It Coriolanus Hamlet Henry IV (Part I) Henry IV (Part II)
Henry V Julius Caesar King Lear Love's Labour's Lost Macbeth
Measure for Measure The Merchant of Venice
A Midsummer Night's Dream Much Ado about Nothing Othello
Richard II Richard III Romeo and Juliet The Sonnets
The Taming of the Shrew The Tempest Twelfth Night The Winter's Tale

G. B. Shaw Caesar and Cleopatra Pygmalion Saint Joan

Richard Sheridan Plays of Sheridan: The Rivals; The Critic; The School for Scandal

John Steinbeck The Grapes of Wrath Of Mice and Men The Pearl

Tom Stoppard Rosencrantz and Guildenstern are Dead

J. M. Synge The Playboy of the Western World

Jonathan Swift Gulliver's Travels

Alfred Tennyson Selected Poetry

William Thackeray Vanity Fair

Flora Thompson Lark Rise to Candleford

Dylan Thomas Under Milk Wood

Anthony Trollope Barchester Towers

Mark Twain Huckleberry Finn

Keith Waterhouse Billy Liar

Evelyn Waugh Decline and Fall Scoop

H. G. Wells The History of Mr Polly The War of the Worlds

John Webster The Duchess of Malfi The White Devil

Oscar Wilde The Importance of Being Earnest

Virginia Woolf To the Lighthouse

William Wordsworth The Prelude (Books 1, 2)

William Wycherley The Country Wife

W. B. Yeats Selected Poetry

English coursework: Prose G. Handley and P. Wilkins
English coursework: Drama and Poetry K. Dowling

All these books are available at your local bookshop or newsagent, or can be ordered direct from the publisher. Indicate the number of copies required and fill in the form below.

Send to: **CS Department, Pan Books Ltd., P.O. Box 40,
Basingstoke, Hants.   RG21 2YT**

or phone: 0256 469551 (Ansaphone), quoting title, author
and Credit Card number.

Please enclose a remittance* to the value of the cover price plus: 60p for the first book plus 30p per copy for each additional book ordered to a maximum charge of £2.40 to cover postage and packing.

*Payment may be made in sterling by UK personal cheque, postal order, sterling draft or international money order, made payable to Pan Books Ltd.

Alternatively by Barclaycard/Access

Card No. | | | | | | | | | | | | | | | | | | |

Signature:

Applicable only in the UK and Republic of Ireland.

While every effort is made to keep prices low, it is sometimes necessary to increase prices at short notice. Pan Books reserve the right to show on covers and charge new retail prices which may differ from those advertised in the text or elsewhere.

NAME AND ADDRESS IN BLOCK LETTERS PLEASE:

....

Name_____

Address_____

_____

_____

_____

8/87